SCRIPTURE •

Why Can't We Stay as We Are?

Why Can't We Stay as We Are?

———

Anthea Dove

DARTON, LONGMAN AND TODD
LONDON

First published in 1991 by
Darton, Longman and Todd Ltd
89 Lillie Road, London SW6 1UD

ISBN 0–232–51924–2

A catalogue record of this book is available
from the British Library

The Scripture quotations are taken from the
Jerusalem Bible, published and copyright 1966, 1967 and 1968, and
the New Jerusalem Bible, published and copyright 1985, by
Darton, Longman and Todd Ltd and Doubleday & Co Inc
and used by permission of the publishers

Cover: *Pot of Geraniums* by Henri Matisse.
National Gallery of Art, Washington; Chester Dale Collection.

Phototypeset in 10/12 Trump by Intype, London
Printed and bound in Great Britain by
Courier International Ltd, East Kilbride, Scotland

Contents

Introduction

⬥

THE WRITINGS OF THE BIBLE – the Scriptures –
are the Word of God. They are of supreme importance
to all Christians and to all who wish to know and
understand the meaning of Christianity. The Bible
should be in every Christian home. Every aspect of
Christian life and worship should reflect in some way
what God says to his people. Catholics have not always
been very good at reading and studying the Bible. In
1965 during the Second Vatican Council a document
on Scripture as the Word of God (*Dei Verbum*) was published. This has had a marked effect in laying the found-
ations for an official programme of encouragement
to Catholics to make the Bible central to their lives.

Much has happened since then. Every public act of
worship has its readings from Scripture. Scripture (both
Old and New Testaments) has a significant place in
all religious education programmes, whether for adults
or for children. The lectionary for the readings at daily
and Sunday Mass covers a large amount of Scripture
during its three-year cycle. Familiar acts of devotion
like the Rosary and the Stations of the Cross have
become far more scripturally based.

The positive value of this is obvious enough. But it
has also meant that many Catholics have been thrown
in at the deep end. They are a little like the Ethiopian

in his carriage on the way home from Jerusalem who
was reading some Scripture. Philip the Deacon heard
him and asked him if he understood what he was
reading. 'How can I', the man said, 'unless I have someone to guide me?' (Acts 8:26–40). Most of us do need
help if we are to understand what we are reading. It is
not that the language of Scripture is particularly difficult; it is rather that its context is so often unfamiliar.

I warmly welcome this series of *Scripture for Living*.
Its particular value is that it helps us to see how Scripture is relevant to our daily lives. There are many
other books for scholars. This series is for ordinary
Christians who treasure Scripture, know for certain
that it is of fundamental importance, but who are not
sure how to make sense of what they read or how to
relate it to their daily lives and experiences.

The pattern of the series is story, bible passage, com-
mentary, reflection and prayer. There is a natural pro-
gression in this. The writings in the Bible (which form
a whole library really) are about people trying to recognise God in their lives. So the context is just everyday
life – the stuff of story. Story leads on naturally to
Scripture because Scripture is itself about life in all its
variety. So it speaks of love and hate, success and
failure, death and resurrection; almost every imagin-
able human failing and strength finds place in it,
simply because it is about real people. The commen-
tary is an aid to understanding. Then, since the ultimate purpose of Scripture is to lead people closer to
God, the text finishes with a prayer which ties together
what has gone before and shows how our daily lives
can be enriched.

The series is ideal for use in groups as well as by
individuals. I wish it every success.

+ DAVID KONSTANT
Bishop of Leeds

Preface

◄——►

MOST OF US FIND IT DIFFICULT to change. If we
feel secure where we are, we naturally resist invi-
tations to step into the unknown or accept new ideas.
'Why can't we stay as we are?' we ask.

Christians, quite rightly, love their traditions and
often hold onto them out of a sense of loyalty. Perhaps
what we need is to see clearly where, however painful
it may be, the familiar ways of doing things have to
be sacrificed in the interests of evangelisation, or
spreading the good news. To take a simple illustration,
those young people who are 'the Church of tomorrow'
will often hear that good news through choruses sung
to a guitar rather than through plain chant, however
beautiful.

All of us need to be open to change *within* because
it is only through openness to the action of the Holy
Spirit that we can grow towards that fullness of life
and love which God desires for us all. Cardinal
Newman said, 'In this imperfect world, to live is to
change; to be perfect is to have changed often.'

Scripture often comes alive for us if we listen or read
with open minds. I hope that those who read this book
will find God speaking to them in the passages I have

chosen, and will be happy to change when that is God's
will for them.

ANTHEA DOVE

Age Concern

—■—

'WHY CAN'T WE STAY as we are?' said Len. 'We're happy here. We've always been happy. We've built this home together, made it what it is. We're not moving, whatever anyone says, and that's final.'

His indignation made him a little breathless and red in the face. Sarah said nothing. She went on with her knitting, calm and quiet. Len waited, knowing her ways well. After a while he said:

'Sarah? You feel the same, don't you?'

She looked up at him then. 'Of course I feel the same', she said. 'You know I do. I love this house, and all the memories. I feel I couldn't bear to leave it. And yet I know we must.'

'But *why*?' asked Len. 'Why can't we stay as we are?'

'Because it isn't right', said Sarah. 'Oh, I know we both dread moving into Meadowlands. For all its fancy name and that smiling matron, we know it's nothing more or less than an Old Folks' Home. I don't want to go there any more than you do, Len.'

'Then how can it be right?' She heard the misery and anger in his voice.

'Look, Len', she said gently, 'it's right because we're not independent any more. The children are worried sick about us. Somebody has to drive us to the doctor, to church, to the shops. My arthritis is getting worse, you've got angina and a gammy leg. I think we just have to face up to it: we can't go on much longer. I'm sorry, Len.'

Len looked at her. He heard the regret in her voice and saw the sorrow in her face. They sat together in silence for a while. Sarah went on with her knitting. He began to feel angry again, not with Sarah, but with life, with God. Why can't we stay as we are? Len thought bitterly. I hate being old and disabled. It's a miserable way to end your life.

◍➞

Yahweh said to Abram, 'Leave your country, your kindred and your father's house for a country which I shall show you; and I shall make you a great nation, I shall bless you and make your name famous; you are to be a blessing!

> *I shall bless those who bless you,*
> *and shall curse those who curse you,*
> *and all clans on earth*
> *will bless themselves by you.'*

So Abram went as Yahweh told him, and Lot went with him. Abram was seventy-five years old when he left Haran. Abram took his wife Sarai, his nephew Lot, all the possessions they had amassed and the people they had acquired in Haran. They set off for the land of Canaan, and arrived there.

(Genesis 12:1–5)

◍➞

Abram was an old man when God called him to leave the land where he lived and go to another country, a strange land which God had promised to show him. Abram (later God gave him the name Abraham, and Sarai he called Sarah) had to make the decision –

should he trust in the Lord and obey him, or should he and Sarai stay as they were? How much easier their lives would have been, how much more comfortable, if they had stayed in their own land!

But Abram believed in God and trusted in him, and so he did what he knew to be right. He took Sarai and his nephew, Lot (as yet Abram and Sarai had no children), his servants and all his possessions, and went to live in the land of Canaan. It was an act of faith.

God rewarded Abram and Sarai. He promised that Sarai would bear a son, thus granting their dearest wish, and told them that their descendants would be as many as the stars in heaven, or the grains of sand on the seashore.

But Abram did not know this when he obeyed God and moved to the land of Canaan.

It's all very well for Abram, you may think. For him it was straightforward; God spoke to him directly. How can we know what God's will for us may be? This is a question which dogs all of us who believe in God and try to do his will.

It is extremely rare for God to speak to us in actual words. Sometimes, when we are faced with big decisions, it seems impossible to know what God would have us do. At other times it seems that our everyday problems have nothing at all to do with God and the Church. This is far from the truth, which is that God is present in every situation. He is there with us when we suffer, he is there even when we sin.

But how do we know what is right?

A young woman called Lucy thought she was happily married until she met Richard. She fell blindly in love with him and he with her. Her whole life was transformed. Richard was wonderful. She thought of him all day long and most of the night. She longed to leave John, her husband, and marry Richard.

Situations like this occur all too frequently. The kind of love Lucy felt for Richard is extremely powerful, and considerations such as the sanctity of marriage that were previously central, no longer seem even relevant.

Lucy, a good Christian, knew very well what the Church's teaching is. In such a situation it is all too easy to dismiss the laws of the Church as out-of-date, the invention of dry old men who know nothing of 'love'.

A more honest and helpful way of discerning what is right is to seek God's will in prayer, not by beseeching him to let us have our own way, but by listening to him in silence, with open hearts. Gradually, if we persevere, we will come to a sense of what is right. Our decision will depend on our integrity, on our understanding of God: his love and his concern and his presence with us. God is not a dry old man.

Supposing that Lucy has tried to do all this. She has refused to be rushed into things. She has asked for God's guidance day after day, and at last come to see that to leave John for Richard would be wrong, wrong not only in the sense of breaking a law, but wrong because of the hurt to John, wrong because she would be betraying herself too, her integrity and all she believes in.

Then Lucy has to face an overwhelming change in her life. She has to give up seeing Richard, and for her it will be like death, like all the lights going out in her world.

This is real bravery, deliberately to accept a painful change for the sake of what is right, as Abram did.

Abram put his trust in God. This, too, we often find difficult. A child is raped, a family wiped out in a car accident. Was this because they didn't have enough trust in God?

Of course not. We don't put our trust in God so that he will prevent dreadful things happening to us. We simply trust that he is there with us, whatever happens, holding us in his love. He is the one who knows when a sparrow falls to the ground and has counted the hairs of our heads.

FOR REFLECTION

1. In your own life, do you ever try to discern God's will when you have to make a difficult decision?
2. Have you ever done something which involved a big change in your life, because you knew it was right?
3. Which of these adjectives would you apply to Sarah, Len's wife: clear-sighted; weak; courageous; unselfish or domineering?

PRAYER

Lord, I lack courage. I lack the insight to know your will for me. Keep me close to you, and help me to grow in understanding so that I may see clearly what is right. Give me strength to accept change when it is necessary for my growth and the welfare of others.

The 'Nobody'

THE PARISH WAS very small. Father James was writing a book, and he combined the two activities, parish priest and author, quite successfully. Then some builders got permission to build a big housing estate on the edge of the village where the church was, and in no time at all the number of Catholics attending Mass had doubled.

One Sunday Father James announced that he had decided to appoint a eucharistic minister. There was a lot of speculation as to who would be chosen for this honour. Some people guessed it would be Ted Phillips, headmaster of the school; others guessed the doctor, who read so well in church, or Sister Gabriel, as she was a nun.

But Father James didn't ask any of these people. He asked Tom Hubbard, who worked for the council sweeping the roads.

Tom was astonished, and dismayed too. 'Oh no, Father', he said, 'you can't mean me. I'm nobody. I'm not good enough. There's plenty of people you could ask as would be more suitable. Please don't ask me.'

'I'm sorry, Tom', said Father James, 'but I've thought a lot about this and prayed hard. I've come to the conclusion that you are the one who would make the best eucharistic minister. I'm sorry, but there it is.'

Tom hung his head and shuffled his feet. After a while he said, 'All right, Father, if you say so.'

Accepting this honour made a big change in Tom's life. He did not lose his humility but he grew in self-confidence. He became eager to know more about the God he was serving, and he gradually took more and more of an interest in the people he visited with Holy Communion. Tom became well-known and respected in the parish, and after some years he was elected chairman of the Parish Council.

He changed his role and his status, but in no way did he change his character, except that he became more devout and more caring for his fellow parishioners.

<hr>

Moses was looking after the flock of his father-in-law Jethro, the priest of Midian; he led it to the far side of the desert and came to Horeb, the mountain of God. The angel of Yahweh appeared to him in a flame blazing from the middle of the bush. 'Moses, Moses!' he said. 'Here I am,' he answered. 'Come no nearer,' he said. 'Take off your sandals, for the place where you are standing is holy ground. I am the God of your ancestors,' he said, 'the God of Abraham, the God of Isaac and the God of Jacob.' At this Moses covered his face, for he was afraid to look at God.

Yahweh then said, 'I have indeed seen the misery of my people in Egypt. I have heard them crying for help on account of their taskmasters. Yes, I am well aware of their sufferings. And I have come down to rescue them from the clutches of the Egyptians and bring them up out of that country, to a country rich and broad, to a country flowing with milk and honey, to the home of the Canaanites, the Hittites, the Amorites, the Perizzites, the Hivites and the Jebusites. Yes

*indeed, the Israelites' cry for help has reached me,
and I have also seen the cruel way in which the Egyptians are oppressing them. So now I am sending you
to Pharaoah, for you to bring my people the Israelites
out of Egypt'.*

*Moses said to God, 'Who am I to go to Pharaoah
and bring the Israelites out of Egypt?' 'I shall be with
you,' God said, 'and this is the sign by which you will
know that I was the one who sent you. After you have
led the people out of Egypt, you will worship God on
this mountain.'*

(Exodus 3:1–12)

Poor Moses! What a shock he must have had. He
worked for his father-in-law, looking after the sheep.
When he encountered God in the burning bush he was
overcome with awe. When God chose him to lead his
people, the Israelites or Jews, out of Egypt, he was
dismayed. He felt totally unequal to what God was
asking of him. It was a task for a great soldier, a great
politician perhaps, someone of shrewd intelligence and
outstanding personality – in short, a leader. Moses was
a simple shepherd. No wonder he didn't jump at the
chance to be the leader of God's people.

And yet, he said yes to this tremendous challenge
and change, as Mary said yes to the angel Gabriel, and
Tom in the story said yes to his priest.

When we read the Bible we may often wonder at
God's choice of people. He chose David, a boy who
looked after his father's sheep, to be the greatest King
of Israel, ancestor of Jesus himself.

He chose Mary, an unknown country girl, to be the
mother of his son.

He chose Peter the fisherman, clumsy, uneducated,

cowardly, impetuous Peter, to be the rock upon which he would build his Church.

How true it is that God's ways are not our ways! For David, and Mary and Peter, the change in their lives was unimaginable. Yet all of them accepted the challenge and the change because of their deep faith and love.

Moses changed. He led God's people through all sorts of difficulties and dangers and became one of the greatest figures in the whole of Scripture. At the Transfiguration (Matthew 17), the two men who appeared with Jesus were Elijah, the great prophet, and Moses. But although his status in life changed so completely, he did not become arrogant or proud. In Numbers 12:3 when Moses had long been the leader of the people, interceding for them with God and teaching them his laws, we read, 'Moses was extremely humble, the humblest man on earth'.

Why do you think Father James chose Tom to be the eucharistic minister rather than the headmaster, the doctor or the nun?

And why did God choose all those unlikely people, Moses, David, Mary and Peter, for such important work? God, unlike most of us, can see into the hearts of men and women. He does not judge by appearances. He knows not only what we think and how we feel, but also what we are capable of, our potential.

Father James was a wise and perceptive man. He could see that there was much more to Tom than most people, and especially Tom himself, realised.

Moses, who had such greatness thrust upon him by God, remained 'the humblest man on earth'. Perhaps this was one of his greatest achievements. Success so often 'goes to our heads', and many people, whose lives are radically changed for the better, from poverty to riches, from insignificance to importance, lose their simplicity and humility along the way. It is sometimes difficult to keep our integrity when the circumstances of our lives change drastically.

Most of us think of ourselves as ordinary people. When we are asked, even by someone we respect very much, to take on something which seems quite beyond us, we feel overwhelmed at the decision we have to make. Often we are simply too scared to take that courageous leap in the dark, to accept so big a change in our lives. It's a risk, and if we are brave enough to take that risk, there's another one ahead of us: the danger that we let our new position give us a false idea of who we really are.

If we are willing to take a risk for God, we can count on him to be there, holding us, as the prophet Hosea says, with leading-strings of love.

FOR REFLECTION

1. Have you ever been asked to do something that seemed beyond you?
2. What is your potential?
3. Do you use the talents and gifts that God has given you?
4. What is the difference between real humility and false humility?
5. Jesus said we should love our neighbour as ourselves. Do you love yourself? Name some of your good qualities.

PRAYER

Lord, teach me to love myself, so that I can love others better. Teach me above all to love you, in response to all that you give me.

If you need me to change, give me the courage to

respond gladly, even when I feel unworthy and afraid. Help me to take risks for your sake, and keep me always true to you and to myself.

Granny Flat

<hr>

JANET LOOKED AT the birthday cards on her mantel-piece. There were only five, but that wasn't what hurt. There was nothing from Sam, her only son. She shook herself crossly.

'Don't be so silly', she said aloud, 'You're sixty years old – it's time you grew up!' After all, she told herself, Sam and Ruth lead such busy lives – they can't be expected to remember an old woman's birthday . . . She busied herself preparing lunch. She had treated herself to a fillet of plaice, followed by a meringue. She knew that Will, who had died two years ago, would have wanted her to celebrate. She had invited Dorothy and Eileen, friends she had known all her life, to join her for supper, but they were both busy with their families.

The loud knock on the door startled her, but when she opened it to find Sam and Ruth standing there, with little Dan, her grandson, she almost cried with pleasure. Sam was carrying Dan and Ruth held an armful of flowers.

They had brought food, food for a feast, a bottle of wine and luxury presents of the kind Janet couldn't afford. After the meal Ruth insisted on washing up, and then, as they sat round the fire drinking coffee, she took an envelope from her pocket and gave it to Janet.

'What is it?' said Janet, nervously looking from the envelope to Ruth. Her daughter-in-law looked shy, uncertain.

'I don't know what you'll think, Janet', she said. 'Treat it as a joke if you like. The last thing we want is to put pressure on you.'

'Pressure?' Janet echoed, thinking, whatever can it be?

She opened the packet and found an ordinary key inside. Puzzled, she looked at Sam who was grinning broadly, and then at Ruth who seemed anxious.

'But what is it? What's it the key to?' Janet asked.

Ruth swallowed. 'We've built an extension to the house, you see. It's a self-contained flat.'

'We thought of letting it', Sam explained, 'but Ruth . . .' He broke off. Ruth was blushing.

'Janet', she said, 'could you, could you think about coming to live with us? I know it's an awful lot to ask, but we'd love it. Please don't say no without thinking about it.'

Janet said nothing. The idea of moving dismayed her. She had lived in the same house for nearly forty years. All her friends were in the village. It was unthinkable.

Then an idea struck her.

'Perhaps you want to go back to work, Ruth?' she said. 'I would look after Dan for you. I'd love that, of course, only . . .'

'Oh no, no!' Ruth interrupted. 'I wouldn't dream of using you like that. I'm not going back to work. I want to bring Dan up myself and we can afford it.'

'Then why . . . ?' asked Janet.

Sam's voice was teasing. 'Mum! You always were a

bit slow on the uptake! It's quite simple – we love
you, we want you with us.'

But Janet was looking at Ruth. To her amazement
she saw tears in her daughter-in-law's eyes.

'Please, Janet', she said, 'do what's best for you. Take
your time to think about it. Your friends must mean
so much to you, but, well – you mean a lot to us!'

After they'd left, Janet sat quietly, thinking to herself: It's been a wonderful birthday – I can't believe it.
And the best thing that's happened is realising that
Ruth really cares for me. Perhaps that's what matters
most. Could I uproot myself and go and live with
them?

*Naomi said to her two daughters-in-law, 'Go back,
each of you to your mother's house. May Yahweh
show you faithful love, as you have done to those who
have died and to me. Yahweh grant that you may
each find happiness with a husband!' She then kissed
them, but they began weeping loudly, and said, 'No,
we shall go back with you to your people.' 'Go home,
daughters,' Naomi replied, 'Why come with me? Have
I any more sons in my womb to make husbands for
you? Go home, daughters, go, for I am now too old to
marry again. Even if I said, "I still have a hope: I shall
take a husband this very night and shall bear more
sons," would you be prepared to wait for them until
they were grown up? Would you refuse to marry for
their sake? No, daughters, I am bitterly sorry for your
sakes that the hand of Yahweh should have been
raised against me.' They started weeping loudly all
over again; Orpah then kissed her mother-in-law and
went back to her people. But Ruth stayed with her.*

Naomi then said, 'Look, your sister-in-law has gone

back to her people and to her god. Go home, too;
follow your sister-in-law.'

But Ruth said, 'Do not press me to leave you and
to stop going with you, for

> *wherever you go, I will go,*
> *wherever you live, I shall live.*
> *Your people will be my people,*
> *and your God will be my God.*
>   (Ruth 1:8–16)

This is an amazing story, unique even in the Old Testament, which is full of interesting and often exciting happenings. Ruth decided to leave her own country, everything and everyone familiar, to go with her mother-in-law to a strange land. This was not the equivalent of a French woman coming to live in England; perhaps a better comparison would be with an English woman going to live among an African tribe with a completely different culture. Ruth was even willing to abandon her own religion. All this is impressive enough, but when we consider that she did it out of love, not for a parent or a child or a lover, but for that most maligned of relations, her mother-in-law, then it is astonishing.

Naomi, Ruth and Orpah had been through a great deal of suffering together and this perhaps drew them close. Orpah, too was willing to go with Naomi to live in a strange land, so we can guess that Naomi (in spite of her rather bitter humour!) was a particularly lovable woman. Even so, there is a difference between being willing to do something and actually doing it, and it was Ruth who took the risk and changed her life drastically with no other motive than that of love.

Jesus left Nazareth and his humble, hidden life, and

completely changed his way of living. He did this for
love of his Father and for love of us, his brothers and
sisters. Those who decide to become missionaries
abroad or workers in developing countries or con-
templatives in remote monasteries are other Ruths;
they too abandon everything familiar out of unselfish
love.

Can you see in your own life, or the lives of others,
examples of people who have changed their lives for
the sake of others? Recently, Pat, a young friend of
mine, told me that she was in love with Johnnie and
that they would soon be getting married. A few weeks
later I saw her looking very unhappy. When I asked
what was the matter, she told me Johnnie wanted to
emigrate to Australia.

'I wouldn't go there to live!' she said. 'What about
Mum and Dad? What about all my friends? I'm not
going. It means we're splitting up – we're not getting
married after all.'

We could say that Pat obviously didn't love Johnnie
enough to make such a big change in her life. We could
also say that Johnnie didn't love Pat enough to stay in
England. In marriage, and all close relationships, there
are often situations where one or the other has to
change. Usually we need to give ourselves time to
think and reflect and pray so that we can discern what
is best, for ourselves and for the other.

FOR REFLECTION

1. Have I ever accepted a big change in my life for
    love of someone else?
2. Could I accept a big change for love of someone
    else?
3. In my marriage/close relationships, do I put myself
    first, or the other person?

4. Make a private list of the people you really love.

PRAYER

Dear Lord, teach me to value the people you give me to love. Teach me to love them as much as I love myself, and without being weak, falsely humble or a 'doormat', to put their needs and interests first.

The Gossip

—⬤—

AS THEY WERE tidying the sacristy after Mass, Betty fished in her capacious bag.

'Look, Father, I've got something to show you', she said, holding up a tiny, fluffy, white garment.

Father Michael smiled at her. 'Well, I'm no expert in these things, Betty', he said, 'but it looks very pretty. What is it?'

Betty laughed. 'Oh Father, you're hopeless', she said. 'It's a matinée jacket for a newborn baby. I've made it for Emma Wright, but she wasn't at Mass.'

Father Michael's face changed. 'No, Betty', he said, 'she wasn't at Mass. She told me she won't be coming any more.'

'What!' Betty nearly dropped the matinée jacket in her surprise. 'But why ever not, the silly girl!'

'Sit down, Betty, and I'll tell you about it', said the priest.

'You see, someone upset her very much. She overheard two people talking about her. One of them said she had no right to flaunt herself the way she did and that she seemed to have no shame.'

'But that's terrible!' said Betty. 'Poor girl, it's hard enough being pregnant when you're not married without having to put up with other people's unkindness!'

'Is that what you really think, Betty?' asked Father Michael.

'Yes . . . yes, of course. Why do you ask?'

'Because I'm afraid it's you who made Betty leave the Church.'

'Oh, no!' Betty looked at him, her face reddening. 'But that's terrible! I think I know what might have happened, Father. Last Saturday morning I was in the sacristy with Sheila. We were having a bit of a gossip.'

'That's right. And Emma came along to see if she could help with the flowers and heard her name being mentioned . . .'

The same afternoon, Betty knocked on Emma's door. When Emma opened it and saw who it was, she almost shut it, but something in Betty's face made her hesitate.

'Emma', said Betty, 'please let me come in. I've come to tell you something important.'

'Come in, then', said Emma rather grudgingly, but she offered Betty the only armchair in her bedsit.

'Emma, I've come to say I'm very sorry. Father Michael told me you overheard me talking about you. I was so stupid, I wasn't really thinking what I was saying, just being malicious. I didn't mean what I said. I'm really fond of you, Emma.'

Emma's face registered disbelief.

Betty took a parcel from her bag and handed it to Emma. She opened it and found the matinée jacket. Her face lit up.

'Oh, Betty, it's beautiful! Did you make it?'

'Yes, I did', said Betty humbly. 'It doesn't make up for what I said, I know, but it does show that I care about you, Emma. Can you forgive me?'

Emma sighed. 'Yes I can, Betty', she said. 'I'll admit it threw me a bit. I thought you were my friend, you see. I mean, if someone like you is against me, what must other people think? That's why I don't go to Mass any more.'

'Oh, Emma, please, could you *try* to come?' Betty pleaded. 'I'll call for you if that would help. And you're wrong you know – most people are much nicer than me.'

Emma smiled for the first time. 'I don't believe that', she said, 'but I'll be here on Sunday morning. Come along if you like, and we'll see if I've got the guts to come with you.'

When you read this story, did you feel more sympathy for Betty or for Emma? What happened was really a blessing for Betty, because it changed her fundamentally. She had thought of herself as a good person, a 'pillar of the church'; she came to realise that she was a sinner, capable of thoughtless cruelty. This humbling experience must have been a significant point of growth in Betty's spiritual life.

⬤══⬤

It happened towards evening when David had risen from his couch and was strolling on the palace roof, that he saw from the roof a woman bathing; the woman was very beautiful. David made enquiries about this woman and was told, 'Why, that is Bathsheba, Eliam's daughter, the wife of Uriah the Hittite'. Then David sent messengers and had her brought. She came to him, and he slept with her ...

David wrote a letter to Joab ... 'Station Uriah in the thick of the fight and then fall back behind him so that he may be struck down and die' ...

Yahweh sent Nathan the prophet to David. He came to him and said:

'In the same town were two men,

one rich, the other poor.
The rich man had flocks and herds
in great abundance;
the poor man had nothing but a ewe lamb,
one only, a small one he had bought.
This he fed, and it grew up with him and his children,
eating his bread, drinking from his cup,
sleeping on his breast; it was like a daughter to him.
When there came a traveller to stay, the rich man
refused to take one of his own flock or herd
to provide for the wayfarer who had come to him.
Instead he took the poor man's lamb
and prepared it for his guest.'

David's anger flared up against the man. 'As Yahweh lives,' he said to Nathan, 'the man who did this deserves to die!' . . .

Then Nathan said to David, 'You are the man. Yahweh the God of Israel says this: 'I anointed you king over Israel; I delivered you from the hands of Saul; I gave your master's house to you, his wives into your arms, I gave you the House of Israel and of Judah; and if this were not enough, I would add as much again for you. Why have you shown contempt for Yahweh, doing what displeases him? You have struck down Uriah the Hittite with the sword, taken his wife for your own, and killed him with the sword of the Ammonites . . .'

David said to Nathan, 'I have sinned against Yahweh'.

(2 Samuel 11:2–4; 14–15, 12:1–5; 7–9; 12)

These extracts from the second book of Samuel are only fragments of the story of David and Bathsheba. David's story is well worth reading in its entirety.

David epitomises what we generally mean by 'the great and the good'. God chose him out of all the Israelites to be their king, and he has been remembered throughout Jewish history for his heroism and holiness. One of the titles given to Jesus himself was 'Son of David'.

And yet this was the man who seemingly without thought committed adultery and murder. Nathan the prophet brought home to him the evil he had done, and the great King David was humbled, acknowledging his sin. He saw himself for what he was, and he changed from being confident in his own virtue and importance, to accepting that he was indeed a sinner.

It is relatively easy for practising Christians to become a little smug. Perhaps it is especially easy in our day when we are confronted in the media by so much that is evil: war, violence, murder, rape, materialism. As Christians we are glad, sometimes proud, to be different, to live by gospel values, to 'shine like stars' and to be a light in our world.

But we have to be very careful to know ourselves well, to understand our own motives. Very often we are 'nice', so that people will *think* we are nice, and we do good not for the sake of Jesus, but because it makes us feel good.

It is a painful and chastening experience for some of us when we discover that we are no better than our non-believing friends, but this experience is also a moment of truth.

Suppose I discover that I am acting only from motives of self-interest when I had all along thought I was serving God. I could be totally discouraged and give up altogether, or I could change. I could begin again, humbly acknowledging my weakness, and see myself as simply an instrument in God's hands trying to act only out of love for him.

If we decide to make a new start, it is important to recognise that we won't achieve our change of attitude and motivation overnight: the process is likely to take a lifetime, but it is well worth persevering.

FOR REFLECTION

1. Do I know myself?
2. Do I see myself as God sees me?
3. Can I be honest about myself?
4. Do I need to change?
5. Do I find Confession, the Sacrament of Reconciliation, helpful?
6. Is a small group helpful for self-discovery?
7. Have you good friends, or a spiritual director, who might help you to understand where you are on your spiritual journey?
8. Betty's 'sin' was one most of us are guilty of at some time or other. We often overlook the importance of the words we speak. How can we use our tongues for *good*?

PRAYER

Lord, only you understand me, the workings of my mind and the needs and longings of my heart. You know me better than my closest friends, better than I know myself. Forgive my foolish ways, and help me to see how I can change.

The Lapsed

DAISY AND CLIFF seemed to live an idyllic life, and
were the envy of their friends. She was pleasant and
pretty; he was good-looking and amusing, successful
in his business. They had one little girl, Susan, and
they lived in a beautiful house on the outskirts of the
town.

Then, one day without any warning, Daisy asked
Cliff for a divorce. She was leaving him and Susan to
go abroad with someone she had met at evening
classes. Cliff was heart-broken. He left his job and for
several weeks looked after his little daughter in a state
of numbness. Then, for months afterwards, he alter-
nated between feelings of anger and deep distress.
Eventually he managed to pull himself together suf-
ficiently to look for a new job. It wasn't easy and when
he at last found something the salary was not enough
to meet his mortgage payments and a wage for Susan's
child-minder. They had to move into rented accommo-
dation in the town.

A few months later Susan was diagnosed as having
leukaemia, and within the year she was dead.

In all the time, since Daisy left him, Cliff had not
been to Mass. In everything he had suffered the Church
seemed irrelevant. Then one day a young priest he had
not met before called to see him. Cliff would not have

invited the priest in, but he had a stammer and he felt
sorry for him. Over a cup of tea the priest asked him
if he would consider coming back to the Church.

'If you would only come back', he said, 'it would
encourage others. If they saw that you, who have suffered so much, still believe in God, it would inspire
people . . .'

Cliff interrupted him. 'But I'm not even sure if I do
believe in God', he said.

The priest didn't seem shocked or even surprised.
Cliff's words did not deter him. 'Please pray about it,
if you can', he said.

People react to suffering in different ways. The process
of grieving follows roughly the same pattern for most
of us: shock, anger, distress – and just when we begin
to feel that at last we're 'getting over it', we are hit by
new waves of distress or anger. It is true that for most
of us, time does heal, but sometimes the process is
very slow.

This whole experience of suffering affects us deeply.
Some people emerge from it bitter and inward-looking,
others attain a new understanding of themselves and
a greater capacity for empathy and compassion. The
most effective counsellors are usually those who have
endured deep sadness in their own lives.

❖

My praises echoed in every ear,
and never an eye but smiled on me;
because I freed the poor man when he called,
and the orphan who had no one to help him.
When men were dying, I it was who had their blessing;
if widows' hearts rejoiced, that was my doing.
I had dressed myself in righteousness like a garment;
justice, for me, was cloak and turban.

I was eyes for the blind,
and feet for the lame.
Who but I was father of the poor?
The stranger's case had a hearing from me.
I used to break the fangs of wicked men,
and snatch their prey from between their jaws.

So I thought to myself, 'I shall die in honour,
my days like a palm tree's for number.
My roots thrust out to the water,
my leaves freshened by the falling dew at night.
My reputation will never fade,
and the bow in my hands will gain new strength.'

(Job 29:11–20)

And now, the life in me trickles away,
days of grief have gripped me.
At night-time, sickness saps my bones,
I am gnawed by wounds that never sleep.
With immense power it has caught me by the clothes,
clutching at the collar of my coat.
It has thrown me into the mud
where I am no better than dust and ashes.

I cry to you, and you give me no answer;
I stand before you, but you take no notice.
You have grown cruel in your dealings with me,
your hand lies on me, heavy and hostile.
You carry me up to ride the wind,
tossing me about in a tempest.
I know it is to death that you are taking me,
the common meeting place of all that lives.

(Job 30:16–23)

Job listened to the opinions and taunts of his friends,
and had long and anguished conversations with God,

but at last he was able to let go of all his resentments
and stand before God in complete humility. This was
the answer that Job gave to Yahweh:

I know that you are all-powerful;
what You conceive, you can perform.
I am the man who obscured your designs
with my empty-headed words . . .

I retract all I have said,
and in dust and ashes I repent.

(Job 42:1–3; 6)

❮❯

The book of Job is unique in the Bible; it is quite
different from all the other books. It is the story of one
man's suffering and how he coped with it, and it raises
the sort of questions that trouble us today, thousands
of years later.

Job's life was turned upside-down overnight. From
being happy, prosperous and healthy, he was bereft of
his children and all his possessions. Then he became
ill with a terrible disease, sickening for others as well
as himself. Job and his wife and his friends ask the
sort of questions we ask when we are hit by tragedy:
Why me? What have I done to deserve this? How can
God let me suffer like this? Is it a punishment for
something I've done? If God is love, how can he allow
such unhappiness and pain? Job and his friends struggle
in vain to find the answer to these questions, just as
for all of us today the problem of suffering remains a
mystery.

Through it all Job holds on to his integrity and his
faith in the Lord, and in the end (although some scholars think the last chapter was added by a later author

who wanted a happy ending) Job's patience and humility are rewarded.

Some people hold on to their faith in God through every kind of suffering and pain. Most of us are weaker; we find that we are angry with God, or that he seems so far away that we are out of touch, we can't pray any more, or hope any more. In this darkness we often fail to understand that however we may feel, God is still there. We may have stopped loving him, but he continues to hold us in his love. And so, when the cloud of our suffering begins to lift, even just a little, then if we turn again to God, he is there waiting for us, full of love and compassion.

From time to time in all our lives, there will be drastic changes, often not of our own making. Coping with such changes is never easy. It demands patience, courage and trust.

Sometimes, of course, it is the other way round. A couple, childless for many years and longing for a baby, suddenly find that the wife is pregnant. A young woman who has given up hope of finding a partner, falls in love and gets married. A man given six months to live by doctors, is healed and lives for twenty years. A young man apparently addicted to drugs and heavily involved in crime, changes his whole lifestyle when he meets a girl who loves him.

Cardinal Newman once said, 'To live is to change'. Certainly, if we want to grow as Christians, we need to accept the changes which disturb our lives.

FOR REFLECTION

1. What big changes can you recall in your life?
2. How did you react to them?
3. What effect did they have on your life?
4. When you have some control over change in your

life, do you tend to be a 'stick-in-the-mud', or do you generally welcome change?

PRAYER

You may like to use this prayer which was written by Reinhold Niebuhr and is used by Alcoholics Anonymous:

God grant me
the serenity to accept the things I cannot change
the courage to change the things I can
and the wisdom to distinguish the one from the other.

Why Can't We Stay as We Are?

'WHY CAN'T WE STAY as we are?' said Bill Forester, thumping the table in his agitation. 'I was baptised in this church, confirmed and married in it. I've served on the altar for sixty years. And I like it as it is. I don't want any changes. We don't *need* any changes!'

One or two members of the Parish Council grunted or nodded in agreement. Father Peter, with some difficulty, kept his mouth shut and a non-committal expression on his face. Rosie Barlow was not so restrained.

'But Bill', she began, 'things are different now . . .'

'Too right they are', said Edith Beales. 'I agree with Bill. There's no sense in changing things for the sake of change. You're right, Rosie, things out there *are* different now. And a sight lot worse, if you ask me.'

'What do you think, Father?' asked Penny Stonebridge.

'Well', said Father Peter, 'the way I see it is this. We do need to change, because like it or not we belong to the society around us. Of course we don't agree with many of their values, but that's not what we're talking about, is it? We're talking about changing a building.'

'Yes', said Penny eagerly, 'that's just it. We want our building to express something.'

Bill Forester snorted. 'Express what?' he asked. 'What do you reckon it expresses now then?'

'Well', Penny glanced shyly at Father Peter, but he smiled encouragingly, 'it's much too focused on the priest for one thing. If we had a round altar, and benches round it in a circle . . .' She hesitated, seeing that Bill's face had gone a vivid shade of crimson and Edith's mouth had fallen open with shock.

There was a buzz of questions and exclamations, mostly spoken in dismay.

'But you couldn't do that!'

'My grandfather made those benches in 1899!'

'Where would you put the statue of St Joseph?'

'You can't be serious!'

'Oh, but I think Penny *is* serious', said Father Peter, 'and I think she's right. Our church should be inviting, welcoming to everyone. It should somehow express the Kingdom of God.'

You may sympathise with Bill and Edith in this story, or you may feel sorry for Rosie and Penny, struggling to convince the others of the need for change.

Tradition is important, and it is insensitive to get rid of things – benches or statues or ways of doing things which others hold dear, without consultation or explanation. Someone's grandfather, who made the church benches in 1899, must have spent months, perhaps years, on this task, and for all we know he did it out of love for God. For people who have worshipped in a certain way for a lifetime with a deep love for their church building as well as for the Church, it can be very upsetting and frightening when big changes are threatened.

On the other hand it is essential for us as Christians

not to be static. The spiritual life is one of continuous change and growth, of openness and adaptation.

Our buildings make statements, so a round church says something quite different from a long narrow church.

◄———►

[Jesus is speaking.]
'You have learnt how it was said: Eye for eye and tooth for tooth. But I say this to you: offer the wicked man no resistance. On the contrary, if anyone hits you on the right cheek, offer him the other as well; if a man takes you to law and would have your tunic, let him have your cloak as well. And if anyone orders you to go one mile, go two miles with him. Give to anyone who asks, and if anyone wants to borrow, do not turn away.

You have learnt how it was said: You must love your neighbour and hate your enemy. But I say this to you: love your enemies and pray for those who persecute you; in this way you will be sons of your Father in heaven, for he causes his sun to rise on bad men as well as good, and his rain to fall on honest and dishonest men alike. For if you love those who love you, what right have you to claim any credit? Even the tax collectors do as much, do they not? And if you save your greetings for your brothers, are you doing anything exceptional? Even the pagans do as much, do they not?'

(Matthew 5:38–47)

◄———►

As a Jew, Jesus was thoroughly versed in the Scriptures. He knew and understood the part of the Bible we call the Old Testament, and used it to speak with authority. In this passage he is changing and adapting the sacred law so that it becomes the fulfilment of his own teachings. He is saying to his disciples, 'This was the law in the Old Testament, but now we need to change'. As a result of his life among us we are asked to love more and to give more.

Let us look at the passage from the Old Testament which he is speaking about:

'If, when men come to blows, they hurt a woman who is pregnant and she suffers a miscarriage, though she does not die of it, the man responsible must pay the compensation demanded of him by the woman's master; he shall hand it over, after arbitration. But should she die, you shall give life for life, eye for eye, tooth for tooth, hand for hand, foot for foot, burn for burn, wound for wound, stroke for stroke.'

(Exodus 21:22–5)

It is clear from comparing the two readings that Jesus wanted the law to express his ideals of love. He asked that we love one another, he came that we might have life in abundance, he wanted our joy to be complete.

The demands Jesus is making in this passage are far from easy. Most people, even those who lead model and blameless lives, would find it very hard to follow these exhortations to the letter. And yet the passage as a whole is an invitation to us to change, to stretch our willingness to serve God in every detail and so to serve our fellows with humility and affection.

How many of us are capable of literally turning the other cheek? And how difficult it is, in the ordinary experiences of life to judge how to be meek and humble without being a doormat for others to walk over, a pathetic non-person.

It is very difficult indeed for most of us to love our enemies. There are usually all sorts of reasons why we say we can't:

'It's not that I mind what he does to me, it's my wife I'm thinking of.'

'I've tried, God knows I've tried, but she says she's sorry and then she goes and does it again.'

'I wouldn't mind, but she seems to think she's so much better than the rest of us.'

'I've tried to see Jesus in him, but how can I when he's so awful?'

And so on.

Loving our enemies is a very real problem that won't go away. Some people say, 'You don't have to like them, you only have to love them', but I find this misleading. If we take the advice of Jesus and pray with sincerity for those who persecute us, then slowly we may come to find that we can love them after all. And once we have succeeded in loving, it is relatively easy to like them as well.

The Old Testament injunctions were exact and legalistic; what Jesus asks of us is a change from that approach. He asks for great generosity and selflessness – it is an ideal for us to work towards.

FOR REFLECTION

1. Could you offer the other cheek if someone struck you?
2. Can you describe a situation in which someone is weak rather than meek?
3. Does the description 'gentle Jesus, meek and mild' fit with your understanding of Jesus?
4. If you had a small son who came home complaining that another child had hit him, what would you say?
5. In the story of the parish council, where did your sympathies lie?

6. How possible (or impossible!) do you find it to love your 'enemies'?
7. Can you pray for your 'enemies'?
8. The sun rises and the rain falls on bad people as well as good. Do you find yourself making judgements as to who is good and who is bad?
9. In what ways do you think you need to change?
10. In what ways do you think your parish/church needs to change?

PRAYER

Lord, help me not to be afraid of change. Help me to see clearly the difference between change for its own sake and change that is necessary. Help me to be willing to let go of my own traditions, even if they are dearly held, when not to do so would block the growth of your Kingdom. Lord, make me always open to your will and your love.

Girl with a Dream

◀━━━━▶

DEIRDRE KNEW what she wanted to do with her
life. She was going to open a shop and sell beautiful
clothes to beautiful people.

Meanwhile, she was studying dress design at a local
college. At the beginning of the summer holidays, her
godmother, Audrey, who was the principal of a school
for disabled children, sent Deirdre a letter. She was
very short of care staff for the children who had
nowhere to go in the holidays, and she wondered if
Dee could spare one or two weeks to come and help.

Dee was rather annoyed. She had already arranged to
spend the holidays working at 'Clobber', a fashionable
clothes shop in the nearby town. But she was very
fond of Audrey and in the end she wrote back saying
she would help at the school for the last two weeks of
her holidays.

When Audrey received Dee's letter she smiled to
herself. How like Dee, she thought. We'll all be back
at school by then, with the staff at full strength! Still,
she concluded, I mustn't look a gift horse in the mouth
and Dee may enjoy it after all.

But Dee did not enjoy it. All the other care staff
seemed devoted to the children. They all wore jeans
and grubby sweaters and had terrible hairstyles. Dee
found it really depressing, and the two weeks passed

very slowly. Then, two days before she was due to leave, Audrey had a phone call from Mrs Carey who led the Mother Teresa Group in the local parish.

'Audrey? You'll never guess what's happened!' she said. 'You know Mother Teresa is in England? Well, she's travelling down to Bristol today and on the way she'll spend a couple of hours with us! I wonder if I could bring her to the school?'

Everyone was excited, except Dee, who felt pretty cool about the whole thing. She watched Mother Teresa carefully. The old nun shook hands with Audrey and smiled in the direction of the staff, and then she began to talk to the children. Everyone watched as she walked round the school hall. She had something to say to every child, and every child responded to her in some way.

Deirdre, standing at the end of the line by Charlotte's wheelchair, suddenly felt very self-conscious. For the first time she realised how out of place she must look with her red fingernails and smart dress. She stood at the end of the line, holding on to Charlotte's chair, waiting for Charlotte's turn.

Mother Teresa knelt down by the chair and smiled at the little girl and took her hand. Charlotte was paralysed from the waist down. She was a chatterbox, and no respecter of persons. 'How does your sari stay on?' she asked, which made everyone laugh.

Then Mother Teresa looked at Dee. She looked right into her eyes for what seemed a very long time, before she went off with Audrey and Mrs Carey.

Dee asked another assistant to take Charlotte, and slipped out into the gardens. She walked a few times round the lawn, and then back into the school, to Audrey's office.

'Audrey', she said, 'I've been thinking. Is there any chance I could come and help here at weekends?'

It sometimes happens that the most unlikely people are called to serve God in a special way. So often it will not be the well-mannered, nicely behaved girl in a convent school who will recognise a vocation to be a nun. Surprisingly, it will be the rumbustious trouble maker, someone with plenty of spirit.

Many of the outstandingly holy people in history have undergone a dramatic transformation. They have been notoriously *unholy* to start with, but ended up as saints and inspiring leaders, men such as Francis, Augustine, Charles de Foucauld. And of course there is St Paul who experienced the most dramatic turn-around of all.

Deirdre changed, her eyes opened in response to what she glimpsed in Mother Teresa: goodness? great-ness? the power of the Holy Spirit?

◆━━━◆

When he went out after this, he noticed a tax collector, Levi by name, sitting by the customs house, and said to him, 'Follow me'. And leaving everything he got up and followed him.

In his honour Levi held a great reception in his house, and with them at table was a large gathering of tax collectors and others. The Pharisees and their scribes complained to his disciples and said, 'Why do you eat and drink with tax collectors and sinners?' Jesus said to them in reply, 'It is not those who are well who need the doctor, but the sick. I have not come to call the virtuous, but sinners to repentance.'
(Luke 5:27–32)

◆━━━◆

Levi, also called Matthew, was a tax collector. It is important to remember that tax collectors in Palestine in the days of Jesus were not the same as those who administer taxes in our own country today. We may feel some animosity towards those who demand money from us, but they are anonymous and impersonal, we don't meet them face to face. Moreover, they are paid a salary like anyone else and there are no 'perks' to the job.

For Jesus, however, in the time when the gospels were written, 'tax-collector' was synonymous with 'sinner' or 'hated one'. This is because the tax collector was free to take for himself a proportion of what he levied as tax. There was a temptation to be greedy and most of them succumbed to it. Zaccheus, for instance, was a tax collector, and terribly unpopular because of the way he dealt with money to his own aggrandisement.

And so it is surprising that Jesus would choose a tax collector to be one of his chosen twelve disciples. It is also perhaps surprising to some that he chose fishermen, four of them: Peter, Andrew, James and John, because by and large fishermen are thought of as simple people without much education or status. We tend not to have great expectations of fishermen.

But a tax collector was something else again. It must have been astonishing and very annoying too for Zebedee and all the other fishermen when the two pairs of brothers dropped their nets and followed Jesus without a backward look, but their astonishment would be as nothing compared to that of Levi's fellow tax collectors (for after all, Levi was onto a good thing), or the bystanders who might have expected Jesus to choose a person of some standing in the community.

There is a deeply moving painting, 'The Call of Matthew' by the Italian artist Caravaggio. It shows Matthew/Levi as a powerful-looking man, richly dressed, with his eye fixed on Jesus and a finger pointing at his own breast. He seems to be saying, incredulously, 'Me?!'. Yet, as Luke says, 'leaving everything, he got up and followed him'.

The next section of the gospel is interesting. Levi did not simply follow Jesus, but in his excitement and joy he gave a party, sharing his fine house and his food. Jesus did not virtuously decline this invitation, and instead was happy to sit down with Levi's friends, good and bad alike. When the scribes and Pharisees criticise and complain, he explains that it is sinners he has come to call to repentance.

It is as though Levi has in one sense changed completely. In one gesture he has abandoned his job, his wealth and his standing to follow Jesus, who only had to say 'Follow me'. But in another sense he has not changed. He does not pretend to be anything other than he is. He follows Jesus, but at the same time invites Jesus into his own world, a world of banqueting and sinful people. And Jesus accepts.

Levi understands that Jesus loves us and accepts us just as we are. He is with us too, in every situation of our lives – at the pub, or the disco, or Bingo, alone in our homes and even when we are sinning. Our spiritual life, our life with Jesus, does not belong in a separate compartment.

Sometimes, someone or something makes such an impact on us that we change: we may be called to enter religious life, to change from working in a bank to being a social worker (though it is important to remember that we may, with equal validity, be called from being a social worker to working in a bank!). Our God moves in a mysterious way, and only he knows what is best for us at a given time. He speaks to us through other people, through books and films, through nature, and in all sorts of other ways. it is up to us to be alert, to listen for his voice, to look for the signs of his calling. One of the surest ways to equip ourselves to be ready when God calls us, in whatever direction, is to give some time to him each day in prayer.

FOR REFLECTION

1. Look in Scripture for others who had a similar experience to Levi's which changed their lives completely: Philip and Nathaniel (John 1), Thomas (John 20), Peter, Andrew, James and John (Luke 5).
2. If Jesus suddenly came to spend a few days with you, where would you take him, and to whom would you introduce him?
3. Has any person – a teacher, a priest, a vagrant, a neighbour – made such an impression on you that you have changed?

PRAYER

Lord, I ask you to help me pray. Fill me with your Holy Spirit so that I may be ready to answer your call, whenever and wherever it comes.

The Prodigal Daughter

———◦———

ANNIE FOUND the note when she got in from work.

'I can't stand this dump any longer. Sorry – Jenny.'

Jenny was sixteen. An only child, she had been no trouble at all to Annie and Brian since the day she was born, as they often said to their envious friends. To Annie's delight, Jenny had decided she wanted to be a nurse like her mother. Her GCSE results were not brilliant, but they were good enough, and she had moved to the sixth-form college with a bunch of her friends, to study for 'A' levels.

It was there that Jenny met Kim, who had come from a different school, and almost at once things began to go wrong. Under the spell of glamorous, exciting Kim, Jenny became a different person. To her parents' helpless dismay, she started smoking and had her nose pierced. All her life she had been perfectly obedient; now she grew defiant. She stopped studying and instead stayed out late every night with Kim.

Even so, the note was a terrible shock. Annie and Brian were stunned, frightened, angry. They contacted the police, but there was no trace of Jenny or Kim, who had not even left a note for her parents.

'I never understood before what it means to have a broken heart', Annie said one night to Brian.

He put his arms round her. 'I know, love', he said, and she looked up to see his tears.

'Perhaps she'll phone', they said.

'Perhaps she'll write', they said.

'Perhaps she'll just come back one day and surprise us', they said.

But Jenny didn't phone, or write, or come back.

At first she and Kim got on well together. They couldn't get jobs or find anywhere to live, but that didn't trouble them too much. Life was an adventure. The first few weeks were warm and sunny, and it was exciting to sleep in the park under the stars. Jenny thought it was wonderful to be free – free from her parents and their ambitions for her, free from school and all its pressures.

The girls soon made friends with other young people. They learnt where they would get free food and the best places for sleeping. Jenny learnt how to beg; without make-up and jewelry she looked innocent and appealing and of the group of friends, she was the most successful at begging.

Jenny didn't often go hungry, and she quickly got used to sleeping without a mattress, but what she didn't like was feeling dirty. She longed for a hot bath and clean clothes. She could never admit to Kim that quite often she felt homesick.

Then Kim met Johnnie and after a few days Jenny realised they were both taking drugs. The change in Kim horrified her and she began to feel afraid. Both Johnnie and Kim pressed her to join in and it was very hard to refuse. One night, Kim began to shout at her, mocking, 'Run home to mummy, baby! You're a coward, Jenny. I don't want you around if you won't join in the fun.'

Jenny walked miles that night, heedless of the heavy rain. Her head throbbed, her throat ached and she felt

utterly miserable. She had just enough money for a
cup of tea or . . . she hesitated outside a telephone box
and finally made up her mind. She went in and dialled,
her fingers shaking so much she could hardly press the
buttons.

They would be so angry. They might put the phone
down. What could she say? 'I'm sorry'? No, it was
much too feeble.

Her mother picked up the phone. 'Hello?'

'Mum . . .', Jenny broke down. She was sobbing too
much to get any words out. Then it was her father's
voice, firm and comforting.

'Jenny, tell me where you are. We'll come for you,
wherever it is.'

Dramas such as the one that occurred in Jenny's family
are sadly seldom heard of nowadays. In most cases
they don't end so neatly and happily. The list of miss-
ing persons is shockingly long; the number of young
people who run away from home to be lost in London
or other big cities is alarming. For the parents of such
children the heart-break, the longing, the dwindling
hope, and, in most cases, the guilt, are painful in the
extreme. The reasons for a child's running away are
usually complex, and often the parents, once they have
got over their initial anger, begin to blame themselves.

Jenny's life changed dramatically twice. She left her
secure home for the adventure of London; she left the
life that demeaned and frightened her to return to the
refuge of home. She was defiant and cocksure; she
became penitent, aware first of her own vulnerability
and then of her parents' loving forgiveness.

He [Jesus] also said, 'A man had two sons. The
younger said to his father, "Father, let me have the

share of the estate that would come to me". So the
father divided the property between them. A few days
later, the younger son got together everything he had
and left for a distant country where he squandered
his money on a life of debauchery.

When he had spent it all, that country experienced
a severe famine, and now he began to feel the pinch,
so he hired himself out to one of the local inhabitants
who put him on his farm to feed the pigs. And he
would willingly have filled his belly with the husks
the pigs were eating but no one offered him anything.
Then he came to his senses and said, "How many of
my father's paid servants have more food than they
want, and here am I dying of hunger! I will leave this
place and go to my father and say: Father, I have
sinned against heaven and against you; I no longer
deserve to be called your son; treat me as one of your
paid servants." So he left the place and went back to
his father.

While he was still a long way off, his father saw
him and was moved with pity. He ran to the boy,
clasped him in his arms and kissed him tenderly.
Then his son said, "Father, I have sinned against
heaven and against you. I no longer deserve to be
called your son." But the father said to his servants,
"Quick! Bring out the best robe and put it on him;
put a ring on his finger and sandals on his feet. Bring
the calf we have been fattening, and kill it; we are
going to have a feast, a celebration, because this son
of mine was dead and has come to life; he was lost
and is found." And they began to celebrate.'

(Luke 15:11–24)

If there was a chart of the top ten Bible stories, it is

quite likely that the story of the Prodigal Son would be Number One. Telling stories was perhaps Jesus' favourite way of teaching those who listened to him. The gospels contain many such stories, and all of them are drawn from the ordinary life experiences of the people of Jesus' country and time. They are always memorable: two thousand years later we often use the phrase 'kill the fatted calf' which comes to us directly from this story of the Prodigal Son.

It is interesting to notice all the details. The father actually runs to meet his erring son. No respectable Jewish father would ever run; he would never show his ankles! But this father cares nothing for etiquette or convention, he only cares to respond to his son with love, hugging and kissing him and organising a party to celebrate his return.

There is a beautiful painting by Rembrandt showing the son kneeling before the father who holds him close. It captures the moving quality of the story Jesus told, and the amazing tenderness of the father to his repentant child.

The Prodigal Son is you and me, all of us who sin. The Greek word used in the New Testament for repentance is *metanoia*, which means a complete turn around. The son was headed in one direction; he saw the folly of his ways, turned round and came home.

The father (who represents God, *our* loving Father) does not simply forgive: he greets the son with abundant joy and love. So it is with us, when we are truly sorry. That is why Confession, the Sacrament of Penance or Reconciliation, is really a sacrament of joy. God not only forgives our sins, he chooses not to remember them. It is as though they had never been. It is hard for us to grasp this reality and we often leave Confession in a sad and solemn mood, even though we have received absolution. But Jesus said, 'There is more rejoicing in Heaven over one sinner that repents than over ninety-nine just persons.'

There are times in all of our lives when we need to repent, to turn away from sin and seek forgiveness. True repentance always involves change.

FOR REFLECTION

1. Do you identify with anyone in Jenny's story?
2. Do you think her parents were right in welcoming her back so unconditionally?
3. Do you identify with anyone in the story of the Prodigal Son?
4. How do you go about repenting?
5. Do you find it hard to forgive?
6. Do you find it hard to understand why anyone would behave like Jenny?
7. Have you ever tried to see Jesus in someone you find it hard to forgive, or to see them in Jesus?

PRAYER

Father, forgive me for my sins, especially my failure to love. I do not want to be like this. Help me in my struggle to change, to be free from the sins which prevent me from living and loving fully. Help me to believe in the reality and depth of your love for me.

The Workaholic

$\bullet\!=\!=\!\bullet$

AT THE END of Mass Father Joe reminded the people that the Methodists were coming to the church hall for a social evening the following Saturday.

'I'd like to make a request', he said. 'Would some kind person volunteer to organise the refreshments? Please let me know if you are willing to do this.'

Moira made up her mind in an instant. She would organise the refreshments. She was the sacristan, and by the time she had put everything away and tidied up, Father Joe was home in the presbytery. When he opened the door in answer to her knock, she smiled and said, 'Father, I'll gladly organise the refreshments on Saturday.'

To her surprise he didn't smile back. 'Thank you, Moira', he said gravely, 'but I don't want you to do it.'

She stared at him, not believing she heard him right. Now he smiled gently. 'Don't be upset, Moira. Come into the study and we'll have a cup of coffee. I've been wanting to talk to you for some time.'

As they sat drinking coffee, Father Joe said, 'Moira, you're becoming a workaholic. You have four young children to look after, and you're an excellent wife and mother, I'm sure. You're the sacristan, you arrange the flowers, you clean the church, you're on the parish council and the justice and peace committee. And now you're offering to organise something else. Tell me, do you ever stop all this "doing" and settle for just "being"? Do you give yourself space and time just to be with God?'

Moira mumbled, 'I say my morning and evening prayers and come to daily Mass, but there just isn't time . . .'

'Exactly!' said Father Joe. 'Don't misunderstand me, Moira, I appreciate all you do for us, but could it be that you've got your priorities wrong? Perhaps someone else, with a little encouragement, could do some of your jobs? Then you would be free to give some time to God, to be still, to listen to him, just to be.'

Moira was silent for a moment. Then she looked straight at Father Joe and managed a smile.

'You're asking a lot, Father', she said. 'You're asking me to change . . . well, I suppose my whole attitude to life! I don't know if I can, but I'm willing to try.'

It was very difficult for Moira to do as Father Joe asked. He made her stop in her tracks and think. She was very popular in the parish, someone everyone could rely on to help. You could count on Moira. She was always busy, cheerful, involved, whether it was scrubbing the church porch, organising a trip to Lourdes or making suggestions to the parish council.

Until Father Joe spoke to her, it had never occurred to her that she was too busy. She thought of herself as someone who served God and her neighbour, but she was so occupied with doing good that she didn't have time to stand still and wonder, to rest in God's presence, to listen and learn from him.

In the course of their journey he came to a village, and a woman named Martha welcomed him into her

*house. She had a sister called Mary, who sat down at
the Lord's feet and listened to him speaking. Now
Martha who was distracted with all the serving, came
to him and said, 'Lord, do you not care that my sister
is leaving me to do the serving all by myself? Please
tell her to help me.' But the Lord answered: 'Martha,
Martha', he said, 'you worry and fret about so many
things, and yet few are needed, indeed only one. It is
Mary who has chosen the better part, and it is not to
be taken from her.'*

(Luke 10:38–42)

People often comment on this story. They say that
they feel sorry for Martha, who, after all, was only
doing her best. On the face of it, Mary seems to have
been lazy, doing nothing to help, enjoying the atten-
tion of their guest. We can imagine Martha, deter-
mined to produce a beautiful meal, getting hotter and
hotter in the kitchen as the dirty dishes piled up, longing for another pair of hands. It's interesting that
Martha didn't ask Mary outright to come and help her
She spoke to Jesus, almost like a cross child telling
tales about her sister.

Why did she speak to Jesus? Why was she so anxious
that the meal should be perfect? Because for Martha,
as well as for Mary, Jesus was not only a good friend
but someone very special. Martha's way of showing
her love and admiration was to make the best meal
she could manage.

I can't help wondering what this meal was. Some
kind of fish, perhaps, or lamb, with all kinds of herbs
and vegetables and fruits. I expect Jesus and Mary
enjoyed it. But left to themselves, would they have
preferred just bread and cheese?

For Mary it was enough just to be with Jesus. She didn't feel the need to impress him; she didn't want to waste time in the kitchen. Being with him was better than anything else.

I sometimes wonder whether Martha changed as a result of what happened. Did she stop being fretful and worrying about little things? Did she try to find time to be with Jesus, and when he wasn't there, in prayer with his father? We don't know. But my guess is that she did change, because we know from later on in the gospels (John 11:20–7) that she had great faith in Jesus and deep love for him.

In Jesus himself we can find the right balance between prayer and action. He was often worn out with teaching and healing and all the demands of the crowds that continually pressed round him. But he found time to go away by himself and pray.

And in our own day, if we look at Mother Teresa of Calcutta or the Little Sisters and Brothers of Jesus, we find that their tremendously exhausting lives are also grounded in prayer: deep, silent communion with God. It is from this that they draw life, strength and love to cope with all that they do.

Do you see yourself as a Martha or a Mary? Perhaps you are like Moira in the first story? Or perhaps your life is so full of problems – money, alcohol, a difficult marriage, illness, loneliness – that you can only live one day at a time, just managing to keep going? If your life is like that, you won't have the energy to spare for good works, and you may not feel able to pray. Even so, it may be helpful if you can, just sometimes, find a space on your own to be still before God.

Probably more people are like Martha than like Mary. But there are those who are so concerned with their prayer life, with their personal relationship with

God or their own salvation, that they give little time
to others. They forget that Jesus said:

> I give you a new commandment:
> love one another . . .
> It is by your love for one another
> that everyone will recognise you
> as my disciples.
>
> (John 13:34)

There are some people who go to daily Mass, and say
their rosary every day and spend long hours in contem-
plation. They may seem to others (and perhaps even
to themselves) to be holy people, but unless they are
also sensitive to the needs of their sisters and brothers,
and are willing to serve them in practical ways, they
are not whole and balanced: in short, they are not
really holy.

Perhaps we all need to look at our own lives and see
how generous we are with the time we give to God
and to one another. We may find a need for change,
and with God's help we may find the courage and
willingness to bring about that change in ourselves.

FOR REFLECTION

1. Who am I most like, Martha or Mary?
2. Do I fret about many things? What sort of things
   in my life is it reasonable to worry about?
3. Am I willing to change?

PRAYER

Dear Lord, I want to use the time you have given me
in the way that pleases you. I ask you to help me to
see clearly where I need to change, and to give me the

courage and perseverance to bring about that change. I ask you to teach me how to be still with you, and how to serve my sisters and brothers with love.

Loyalty

PHILIP CHASE and Hugh Preston were best friends almost from the day they could speak. As little boys, they spent all their free time together, and when they were nine they cut their fingers and marked each other's foreheads with the mingled blood and swore to be true to each other forever.

When they were thirteen they were sent to the same boarding school where they supported each other in many a quarrel and fight.

When they were fifteen something very upsetting happened. Mrs Fletcher, the headmaster's wife, was growing roses for display in a local show. She checked them for greenfly at eight-thirty one evening. When she walked round the garden with her husband at nine-fifteen, the roses had all been decapitated.

Of course no one owned up, but after a few days someone hinted to Mr Fletcher, the headmaster, that he had seen Philip Chase crossing the lawn at about that time. Philip was summoned to the headmaster and he explained that at the time in question he was smoking with his friend, Hugh, in the potting shed behind the greenhouses.

Hugh was sent for. As he went into the headmaster's room he saw Philip sitting in a corner with bent head.

Hugh was afraid of Mr Fletcher, and even more afraid of his parents, so when the head said, 'Chase tells me that on Saturday evening you and he were smoking in the potting shed. Is this true?'

Hugh panicked. 'No, sir', he said, 'I don't smoke. I've never been to the potting shed.'

'Very well, you can go', said the headmaster, turning to Philip. As Hugh left the room, he nerved himself to look at his friend. Philip, white-faced, looked at him steadily, until Hugh had to turn away.

He ran to his room and flung himself on the bed, crying. What else could he have done? He couldn't have owned up – Fletcher would have beaten him and his parents would have been more than furious.

But what about Phil? Why had he told about the potting shed? Suddenly he felt blood rush into his face. Surely, surely, nobody would have accused Phil of cutting down Mrs Fletcher's roses? And into his mind came the memory of the day, so many years ago when they had sworn undying loyalty.

Hugh ran back to the headmaster's study and burst in, sobbing, as Philip was being caned.

'No, no, stop!' Hugh cried. 'Sir, I told a lie. I'm sorry. Phil told the truth. We *were* in the potting shed . . .'

Hugh was only a child when he lied to the headmaster, but as adults we also sometimes lie out of fear, especially if we are unexpectedly accused of something and don't have time to think.

Because of his love for Philip, Hugh was able to change, to go back and own up to his lie.

All sorts of questions arise when we read this story. What sort of person would have cut off the heads of roses? What was the headmaster's relationship with his boys like? What were Hugh's parents like? Does corporal punishment do any good, or any harm?

Hugh was a very frightened boy but he was also very courageous. It was a really brave act to go back into the headmaster's study. Sometimes we confuse being afraid with cowardice. On the contrary, if we have no fear, then we cannot be courageous.

<hr>

After psalms had been sung they left for the Mount of Olives. Then Jesus said to them, 'You will all lose faith in me this night, for the scripture says: I shall strike the shepherd and the sheep of the flock will be scattered, but after my resurrection I shall go before you to Galilee.' At this, Peter said, 'Though all lose faith in you, I will never lose faith'. Jesus answered him, 'I tell you solemnly, this very night, before the cock crows, you will have disowned me three times.' Peter said to him, 'Even if I have to die with you, I will never disown you' . . .

Meanwhile, Peter was sitting outside in the courtyard, and a servant-girl came up to him and said, 'You too were with Jesus, the Galilean'. But he denied it in front of them all. 'I do not know what you are talking about' he said. When he went out to the gateway, another servant-girl saw him and said to the people there, 'This man was with Jesus, the Nazarene'. And again, with an oath, he denied it, 'I do not know the man'. A little later the bystanders came up and said to Peter, 'You are one of them for sure! Why, your accent gives you away.' Then he started calling down curses on himself and swearing, 'I do not know the man'. At that moment the cock crew, and Peter remembered what Jesus had said, 'Before the cock crows you will have disowned me three times'. And he went outside and wept bitterly.

(Matthew 26:30–4; 69–75)

After the meal Jesus said to Simon Peter, 'Simon, son of John, do you love me more than these others do?' He answered, 'Yes, Lord, you know I love you.' Jesus said to him, 'Feed my lambs.' A second time he said to him, 'Simon, son of John, do you love me?' He replied, 'Yes, Lord, you know I love you.' Jesus said to him, 'Look after my sheep.' Then he said to him a third time, 'Simon, son of John, do you love me?' Peter was upset that he asked him for the third time, 'Do you love me?' and said, 'Lord, you know everything; you know I love you.' Jesus said to him, 'Feed my sheep.'

(John 21:15–17)

◆━━◆

Many people find the character of Peter endearing. There is something appealing about his impetuousness, the way he charges into things without stopping to think. There are several instances of this in the gospels. In Matthew 24:24–31, Peter sees Jesus walking across the water and jumps into the lake to imitate him, but almost immediately starts to sink. And in John 21:4–8, the disciples in their fishing boat see someone on the shore. John says, 'It is the Lord!', and at these words, Peter, 'who had practically nothing on, wrapped his cloak round him and jumped into the water'. There is something attractively foolish about Peter.

But probably what chiefly endears us to this disciple is the fact that we can easily identify with him in his weakness. Who among us, in similar circumstances, would have been brave enough to admit that we were friends of Jesus? Most of us are cowards at bottom, especially when we're faced with a panic situation. And yet, though in all probability we share Peter's weakness, we are glad to read that he wept bitterly in remorse.

It is surprising as well as strangely comforting that Jesus chose this weak, foolish, bumbling, uneducated man to lead his flock. There is a solemnity about the repeated questions of Jesus that makes this occasion a consecration.

Peter changed. Somehow, through the experience of cowardice and betrayal, shame and repentance, above all through his knowledge of the resurrection of his Lord, he became a different person. He began truly to love Jesus. In spite of his shortcomings, he came to possess the one quality necessary to fit him to be the first Christians' leader. 'Lord, you know everything', he says, 'you know I love you.'

It is a question we may well ask ourselves: do we love Jesus? Or do we just pay lip-service to the doctrines of our Church? How real is Jesus to us? And when we pray, are we conscious of praying to God the Father, Jesus, or the Holy Spirit?

It is, of course, impossible to love someone deeply unless they are frequently in our thoughts. In our language the word 'love' has become almost meaningless, because we use it so often and give it such a variety of applications. 'I love bananas', 'I love my fiancée', 'I love my work', 'I love my children'. It's the same word, but it means something different in each sentence.

The love of Jesus which Peter had was the basis of his whole way of living: because of it he was able to triumph over his own weaknesses and failings. Peter's response to the love of Jesus was to love him in return, and this love equipped him to follow the central command of Jesus: 'Love one another'.

When we are in a position to choose leaders we look for all sorts of qualities. Jesus only asked for one.

FOR REFLECTION

1. Do you think Peter changed? Or do you think Jesus chose him in spite of his failings and weaknesses?
2. Do you think you are capable of change? We know that God loves us *as we are*. Do we, therefore, *need* to change?
3. What qualities would you look for in a bishop or other Christian leader?
4. Do you really love Jesus? If you do, what difference does it make to the way you live?

PRAYER

Lord Jesus Christ, help me to change. Help me to become the person you want me to be. Let me change from centring my life on myself to focusing it on you instead, and let my love for you grow ever deeper and stronger.

Too Old?

———

NORAH WAS WASHING UP after the prayer meeting when Dennis Brown approached her.

'Oh, Norah', he said, 'I've been looking for you everywhere. There's something I want to ask you.'

'Yes?' said Norah, smiling and handing him a tea towel. 'What is it then?'

'I wanted to ask you if you'd be willing to help with the young people', Dennis said, 'the sixteen-plus group. We need somebody badly and I think you'd be ideal.'

'Dennis!' Norah laughed, 'you've got to be joking! Me? Ideal? How can you possibly think that? There's no way I'd be any use with young people – I'll be drawing my pension soon! I'm much too old.'

'What difference does age make?' Dennis asked. 'It doesn't matter to me, or the young people, how old you are. What does matter is the kind of person you are. I just know you'd be the right person to help us.'

'Dennis, I couldn't', said Norah. 'I would feel so embarrassed, so useless . . .'

'Look', he persisted, 'on Friday night there's going to be a meeting in the school hall. All the young people will be there, and Penny and myself. Why not come along and see how you feel?'

On Friday night walking towards the school hall, Norah found she was trembling. As she drew near she could see that there were a great many young people talking and laughing together. She stood still, thinking, I can't face it. They'll laugh at me, or else ignore me.

She was about to turn round and go home when someone touched her arm. She turned to find Angela, who had lived next door to her until she was six. Now she was quite grown up, lively and attractive.

'Norah!' she exclaimed, 'I was so pleased when Dennis told me you'd be coming along.' She took Norah's arm. 'Come on, now, or we'll be late. Oh, it will be great to have you with us.'

Norah let herself be dragged forward. If I can stay with Angela it may not be so bad, she thought. But as she stepped through the door into the crowded room, she felt numb with fright. Immediately the young people nearest the door hurried over.

'Hi, Angie!' someone said, and everyone greeted Angela with smiles.

'This is Norah', Angela said, 'she's come to help.'

'That's nice!' said a girl with red hair.

'It's really very good of you', added a boy with long dark hair and ear-rings.

They seem to mean it, Norah thought, they seem to accept me.

Just then a whistle blew, and everyone stopped talking and turned to look at the far end of the hall where Dennis was standing.

'Hello, everyone!' he said. 'I hope you're all going to enjoy this evening. The lady over there with Angie and Tom is Norah. She's very kindly agreed to come along and help us.'

All the eyes in the room focused on Norah. She tried to smile, and when Angela put her arm around her the smile was real. After that there was a good deal of praying and singing. When everybody stopped for coffee, Dennis came over to Norah.

'You're doing really well, Norah', he said. 'Obviously you're a natural for this sort of thing. I hope you won't mind if I ask you to come again?'

Age matters to most of us, most of the time. Norah felt very anxious because she thought she was too old to be of any use to the young people. When we are in our teens we long to grow up, and almost as soon as we *are* grown up we begin to feel old! Age, and appearance too are relatively unimportant, although the advertisements which bombard us would have us believe that the only way to be is young and beautiful.

God judges people differently; he knows the secrets of our hearts. And perceptive people, like Dennis in the story, are often well able to judge a person's real potential. However, it was Norah, not Dennis, who had to make the decision about whether to take on something which seemed to her to be overwhelmingly difficult. Taking the opportunity to serve God in this way involved Norah in a big change — a change of attitude towards both herself and others.

The word of Yahweh was addressed to me, saying,

> *'Before I formed you in the womb I knew*
>   *you;*
> *before you came to birth I consecrated you;*
> *I have appointed you as prophet to the*
>   *nations'.*

I said, 'Ah, Lord Yahweh; look, I do not know how to speak: I am a child!'

> *But Yahweh replied,*
> *'Do not say, "I am a child".*
> *Go now to those to whom I send you*

> *and say whatever I command you.*
> *Do not be afraid of them,*
> *for I am with you to protect you –*
> *it is Yahweh who speaks!'*

Then Yahweh put out his hand and touched my mouth and said to me:

> *'There! I am putting my words into your mouth.*
> *Look, today I am setting you*
> *over nations and over kingdoms,*
> *to tear up and to knock down,*
> *to destroy and to overthrow*
> *to build and to plant.'*

(Jeremiah 1:4–10)

When God tells Jeremiah he has appointed him as prophet to the nations – a terrifying prospect for one so young and inexperienced – Jeremiah objects strongly. He is sure that apart from anything else he is too young.

God is not angry with Jeremiah; he speaks quite tenderly and shows that he understands how Jeremiah feels: 'Do not be afraid of them, for I am with you to protect you'.

But God is quite firm; he will not take no for an answer.

Jeremiah had a terribly hard life in the service of God. He had continually to be a prophet of doom and naturally became very unpopular. For example, he was once let down to the bottom of a well and left to die.

At one point he says to God:

You have seduced me, Yahweh, and I have let myself be seduced;

You have overpowered me: you were the stronger.
I am a daily laughing stock,
everybody's butt.
Each time I speak the word, I have to howl
and proclaim 'Violence and ruin!'
The word of Yahweh has meant for me
insult, derision, all day long.
I used to say, 'I will not think about him,
I will not speak in his name any more'.
Then there seemed to be a fire burning in my heart,
imprisoned in my bones.

(Jeremiah 20:7)

Sometimes, like Jeremiah, we too feel 'a burning in
our hearts'. There is an echo of this in the life of John
Wesley, the great Christian preacher and founder of
Methodism. After a long period of doubt and con-
fusion, he records how one day he felt 'a strange warm-
ing of the heart'. From then on he never wavered in
his convictions, and, again like Jeremiah, he spent a
long and often troubled life in the ardent service of
God.

When our hearts burn within us, as did those of the
disciples on the road to Emmaus, when Jesus, unrecog-
nised, was walking with them, we can face challenge
and change with new courage.

Often when a friend is asking us to do something
we don't want to do, we step back and say no. We feel
inadequate; too young, perhaps, like Jeremiah, or too
old, like Norah; not clever enough, perhaps, or too
busy. Sometimes these reasons are only excuses; sometimes they are genuine but even so are not really an
obstacle in the way of our doing what is needed.

Many of us run away from challenges, from commit-
ment, from change. It may be that we are cowardly, or
lazy, or too concerned with what others may think.

On the other hand, there are people who eagerly say yes to everything, when in truth it would be more humble and more just to say no. In love of God we gladly give him our lives, but what sort of lives are we offering? Is the life I offer God cowardly, lazy, self-indulgent? Is it restless, stressed, exhausted, unpeaceful?

As in all things there has to be a balance. But if it is ever given to us to recognise the heart's burning, then as those who love God, we have no choice.

FOR REFLECTION

1. Have you ever experienced a 'burning of the heart', or an absolute conviction that something was right? Can you describe how it was?
2. Are you someone who says yes too often because you find it difficult to say no?
3. Are you someone who opts for safety and security, rather than taking risks?
4. Do you think/feel that you have done enough in your life?
5. If you were convinced that it was what God wanted you to do, how willing would you be to change: your job; the place where you live; some of your attitudes; some of your behaviour?
6. Could you have done what Norah did?
7. In what ways do you think Norah's life would change when she became involved with young people?

PRAYER

Dear Heavenly Father, you know me through and through. (You may like to read Psalm 139 here.) You know what my answer should be when something is asked of me. Help me to grow in wisdom and openness so that I always recognise and answer a call that comes from you.

Another Way of Seeing

'SAM IS A GOOD BLOKE', said Paul to Ron and Kitty, as Sam left the room.

The three friends were drinking coffee in the church hall after Mass, along with a lot of other people. A few moments earlier, the parish priest, Father Robert, had asked for quiet.

'We've just heard that Martin Green, who was going with the handicapped children to Lourdes next week, has appendicitis', announced Father Robert. 'I've been asked to find out if there's anyone here who would be willing to take his place.'

There was silence, quite a long silence. Then Sam spoke quietly. 'I'll go, Father', was all he said.

'Good man', said the priest. 'Come over to the presbytery now and I'll fill you in with all the details.'

Paul was looking thoughtfully after Sam. 'You seemed surprised when you said that about Sam, Paul', said Kitty. 'Don't you like him, or something?'

Paul hesitated. 'I'm not sure if it's a question of liking', he replied. 'To be honest, I suppose I've been prejudiced against him all this time because he's been in prison. It's funny, I didn't think I was prejudiced. I used to feel it towards gays and black people, but I've got over that. It comes as quite a shock to realise

you're not as tolerant and open as you thought you
were.'

Kitty grinned. 'Well, we all keep on learning. I
reckon I'm not prejudiced either, but you should hear
the way I go on about snobs!'

'I'm glad you feel differently about Sam, though',
Ron said. 'I really admire the man. Just now when
Father asked someone to volunteer for Lourdes, I felt
I ought to offer to go. I can take holidays any time I
like and I could easily afford it. But I didn't want to.
Young Sam is practically on the breadline and he's not
entitled to much in the way of holidays, but he's going.
I take my hat off to him.'

'Me too', said Paul and Kitty in unison.

It was quite a small incident that made Paul see things
differently and realise he had a prejudiced attitude
towards Sam.

All of us are guilty at times of making judgements
on others, and some Christians are particularly harsh
on those they judge to be morally unworthy, such as
criminals and sexual deviants. This is largely due to
our ignorance and fear.

Any kind of prejudice, whatever it is, or whoever its
victim is, needs to be recognised and dealt with.

In order to get rid of prejudice, we need to be open-
minded, non-judgmental and aware of the plank in our
own eyes. We need to feel interest in and concern for
everyone we meet, and to be wary of putting a label
on anyone. Without prejudice, we will find ourselves
changed people: more tolerant, more humble and more
ready to befriend those who come our way.

*When the sixth hour came there was darkness over
the whole land until the ninth hour. And at the ninth*

*hour Jesus cried out in a loud voice, 'Eloi, Eloi, lama
sabachthani?' which means, 'My God, my God, why
have you deserted me?' When some of those who stood
by heard this, they said, 'Listen, he is calling on
Elijah'. Someone ran and soaked a sponge in vinegar
and, putting it on a reed, gave it to him to drink
saying, 'Wait and see if Elijah will come to take him
down'. But Jesus gave a loud cry and breathed his
last. And the veil of the Temple was torn in two from
top to bottom. The centurion, who was standing in
front of him, had seen how he had died, and he said,
'In truth this man was a son of God'.*

(Mark 15:33–9)

All four gospels, Matthew, Mark, Luke and John,
describe the crucifixion of Jesus, and each one is different. This does not mean that any particular gospel is
more accurate than another, or that somebody got it
wrong! When we read all four accounts, our picture of
the dying Jesus is greatly enriched. For example, St
Luke records that Jesus said from the cross, 'Father,
forgive them; they do not know what they are doing',
and St John tells us that seeing his mother and the
disciple he loved standing near his cross, Jesus said to
his mother, 'Woman, this is your son'. Then, to the
disciple, he said, 'This is your mother'.

St Mark's is perhaps the starkest description. The
ultimate suffering of Jesus was not the terrible physical
pain or the cruel jeers of the bystanders or his desertion
by most of his friends. It was the feeling that his father,
God, was not there with him. This was the worst he
had to bear.

The centurion was not really involved except that it
was his duty to stand by the crucified. It is difficult to

imagine a more unpleasant job. Being a Roman he would not have been concerned with the charges made against the criminals he stood guard over: blasphemy against the God of the Jews would have meant nothing to him. However, he must have been aware that crucifixion was the most degrading and agonising of deaths, and that those who were given this dreadful punishment were judged to be the vilest of men.

He saw Jesus die, and he saw how he died. He heard the words he spoke and saw the anguish in his face. The centurion, was changed, changed because he saw the truth. Jesus was no criminal, no ordinary man either – 'Truly this man was a son of God'.

Blinkers fell from the eyes of Paul in the story, and from the eyes of the centurion at the foot of the cross, when they realised the truth. Sam was a good man; Jesus was truly a son of God, whatever meaning these words held for a Roman officer. Quite often our attitude to someone changes when we discover their real worth. A woman we had always thought of as selfish turns out to be a great support when we are in trouble, or a young man we had imagined to be timid and feeble shows a good deal more courage than we have ourselves. We change, then, when we find out the truth. How much better it would be if we could change *now*, throw away our prejudices and judgmental attitudes and accept people unconditionally as our Father accepts us.

It can help if we try to remember that the Holy Spirit makes his dwelling in each of us who are baptised, that Jesus himself is within us when we receive him in Holy Communion.

And yet, to be realistic, we can see only too clearly that so-and-so, a regular communicant, is the most malicious gossip in the parish. I may know this for a fact; what I may not know is *why* so-and-so behaves

in this way, or what other qualities he or she possesses.
I may realise even less clearly the faults I have myself.
Jesus said, 'Do not judge and you will not be judged'.

We are not able to see as God sees. We are not able
to understand all the factors which make a person
what he or she is. It is when we come to recognise
that we *are* prejudiced and judgmental that there is
hope for change.

FOR REFLECTION

1. What are your prejudices?
2. Have you ever changed your opinion about people?
3. Do you listen to other people's judgements, and is
    your own judgement coloured by them, or are you
    able to 'take people as you find them'?
4. Do you have any friends who have been in prison?
5. What is your attitude to people with AIDS?
6. Which is easier, to change the low opinion you
    have of a person to a good opinion, or to change
    yourself so that you don't make any judgements
    on people?
7. What might Paul have done as a result of his experi-
    ence?
8. What might the centurion have done as a result of
    his experience?
9. For Jesus, the worst part of his suffering was the
    feeling that his Father had abandoned him. Have
    you, or someone close to you, endured that kind
    of deep depression where God seems absent?

PRAYER

Lord, change me. Help me to rid myself of precon-
ceived ideas about people. Help me to get free of all

my prejudices. Help me to see myself as you see me, and to see others in the same light.

Courage

◄═══►

JEFFREY BUCHANAN was surprised and delighted to be invited to join the company's board. At the same time he was pretty sure that he had been chosen not for any outstanding ability but because he was the grandson of the founder of Buchanan's.

He felt particularly intimidated by his uncle, Frederick, the chairman of the board, and the first two meetings were an ordeal. He was the youngest partner by twenty years and felt inadequate and foolish, so he said nothing at all. The third meeting was proceeding like the others when something very strange disturbed the partners. From the next room came the sound of people singing, loud enthusiastic singing, the words of which were quite clear: 'Jesus, beautiful Saviour . . .'

Jeffrey only just managed to stop himself laughing. The chairman, red-faced, leapt to his feet, thumping the table.

'I'm not having this!' he shouted. 'It's that fool Harrington. He's started a Christian Society, *in our firm*, can you imagine it? I'm not having that hideous noise disturbing our meeting!' He stomped out and a few seconds later the singing stopped abruptly.

Later, Jeffrey went to look for Frank Harrington.

'I'm sorry about this morning, Frank', he said.

'What's going to happen? Will you have to give up your meetings?'

Frank smiled. 'Oh, no', he said, 'not on your life. It was just unfortunate we were next to the boardroom. It was twelve-thirty, you see, our lunch hour. We didn't know there was a meeting, so we're going to meet down in the cellars in future, out of harm's way.'

At Jeffrey's fourth board meeting the partners were discussing redundancy. The chairman was looking at a list of names. 'Oh, yes, Frank Harrington', he said. 'He'll have to go.'

Jeffrey cleared his throat. 'Excuse me, sir', he said, 'I'm sorry, but could you explain why Frank has to go?'

'He's a trouble maker', the chairman answered. 'He started this silly Christian thing. Didn't even ask my permission. I don't like that sort of thing in my factory – it only leads to trouble.'

'But he's a very good worker and he's been with us a long time. He's got five children, too, and at his age it will be difficult . . .'

The chairman interrupted, smiling indulgently at Jeffrey. 'My dear boy', he said, 'we can't let sentimentality come into these things. When you've had my experience you'll think differently, mark my words.'

The Christian Group had a party in the factory cellar for Frank, the night before he was due to go. They enjoyed a shared supper and then began to sing. After the second hymn someone slipped in, almost unnoticed, but not quite.

Frank went up to Jeffrey, trying to conceal his surprise. 'Hello, Mr Buchanan', he said. 'Welcome to the group!'

'Well, thanks, Frank', said Jeffrey, 'but call me Jeff. I came to say goodbye, and thanks for all you've done.'

It is easy to sympathise with Jeffrey. It needs quite a

lot of courage to speak out when we are in a minority, especially when we are the only one who thinks differently, and, as in Jeff's case, there is someone in authority watching our every move. Perhaps Jeffrey would have been 'wiser' to ignore Frank and his Christian Society, to keep silent when Frank was condemned to redundancy, and to wash his hands of any association with them. But because he was drawn to the Christian Society, and realised the injustice that was being done to Frank, he felt compelled to risk being ridiculed, and in doing so found himself changing into a more confident person.

◆━━━◆

There was one of the Pharisees called Nicodemus, a leading Jew, who came to Jesus by night and said, 'Rabbi, we know that you are a teacher who comes from God, for no one could perform the signs that you do unless God were with him'. Jesus answered.

'I tell you most solemnly,
unless a man is born again from above
he cannot see the Kingdom of God'.

Nicodemus said, 'How can a grown man be born? Can he go back into his mother's womb and be born again?' Jesus replied:

'I tell you most solemnly,
unless a man is born through water and the Spirit,
he cannot enter the Kingdom of God:
what is born of the flesh is flesh;
what is born of the Spirit is spirit.
Do not be surprised when I say:
you must be born from above.
The wind blows wherever it pleases;
you hear its sound.

*but you cannot tell where it comes from or where it
  is going.
That is how it is with all who are born of the Spirit.'*

(John 3:1–8)

*The police went back to the chief priests and Pharisees
who said to them, 'Why haven't you brought him?'
The police replied, 'There has never been anybody
who has spoken like him'. 'So' the Pharisees answered,
'you have been led astray as well? Have any of the
authorities believed in him? Any of the Pharisees?
This rabble knows nothing about the Law – they are
damned.' One of them, Nicodemus – the same man
who had come to Jesus earlier – said to them, 'But
surely the Law does not allow us to pass judgement
on a man without giving him a hearing and discover-
ing what he is about?' To this they answered, 'Are you
a Galilean too? Go into the matter, and see for yourself: prophets do not come out of Galilee.'*

(John 7:45–52)

*After this, Joseph of Arimathaea, who was a disciple
of Jesus – though a secret one because he was afraid
of the Jews – asked Pilate to let him remove the body
of Jesus. Pilate gave permission, so they came and
took it away. Nicodemus came as well – the same
one who had first come to Jesus at night-time – and
he brought a mixture of myrrh and aloes, weighing
about a hundred pounds.*

(John 19:38–9)

The cloak and dagger (or at any rate the cloak!) twist
in the story of Nicodemus is intriguing. It also brings

home to us how dangerous it was to be associated with Jesus. It is clear that Nicodemus was afraid of his fellow Pharisees and yet he was attracted to Jesus. This attraction caused him to overcome his fear gradually by speaking out, and then by declaring himself openly with his generous posthumous gift. He changed in the way that so many of us change – not by a sudden conversion, but by a gradual struggle.

It is interesting that although Nicodemus was not a committed disciple of Jesus (at the beginning of John's gospel), it was his privilege to receive the teaching of our Lord on what is perhaps the most wonderful change of all – that of being born anew.

For Nicodemus, it was dangerous to confess to sympathy with Jesus. There is no danger for us, at least in this country, in admitting that we are Christians, but even so, in certain environments, we often find it very difficult. How hard it is to stand up and be counted!

And looking at it from a different perspective, don't we, who see ourselves as 'normal' or 'right', make it twice as difficult for those who long for the courage to say, 'I am an alcoholic', or 'I am a lesbian', or 'I have AIDS'. For this reason many people live furtive, frightened lives, or go along with the crowd because they cannot face the judgement that will fall on them if they say what they really think.

To change, from being like Jeff at the beginning of the first story, or Nicodemus who 'came by night' in John's gospel, into being the sort of person who can openly declare where their allegiance lies, requires considerable courage. For the naturally timid it is difficult in the extreme.

It is so comfortable to be accepted, to be thought of as nice and agreeable – why upset the apple-cart; the board meeting; the Sanhedrin? Anything for a quiet life, thinks Jeff, thinks Nicodemus. But then they are challenged to speak the truth, and if they love enough, they will do it. It is the kind of change in ourselves that many of us are called to make.

FOR REFLECTION

1. How did you feel when you first read that Nicodemus 'came by night'?
2. Have you ever engaged in stealthy actions for the sake of something you believed in but were too afraid to declare openly?
3. Are you sometimes shy of admitting that you are a Christian? If so, would you like to change? How would you go about changing?
4. Sometimes people say, 'She's too old to change now'. John is a retired butcher. At the age of sixty-one he wanted to write to his sons to tell them how much he loved them, so he learnt to read and write. Apart from his new skills, in what way do you think John's life has changed?
5. Do you consider yourself to have been born again?

PRAYER

Heavenly Father, give me a deeper trust in your love so that I may have the courage to change when you need me to be different. Fill me with the love that casts out fear, and let me never be ashamed to tell others of my faith in you.

Stick-in-the-Mud?

COLIN WAS HIGHLY RESPECTED in the parish. He was active in all sorts of ways. He cut the grass in the churchyard, taught catechetics to the children who didn't attend Catholic schools, and played the organ. He was also a good friend of the parish priest and they played golf together.

One Sunday as they walked home from Mass, Jane, his wife glanced anxiously at Colin. It was so unlike him to be angry, and with Father John of all people. 'I don't understand why you're so upset, Colin', she said gently.

'Upset! I'm more than upset!' Colin was almost shouting. 'I'm angry and confused. I've always like Father John and admired him, and God knows I'm no stick-in-the-mud. I've gone along with all the changes, even when it's been difficult, but this is the end. You won't see me at his precious Christian Unity Service!

'I always go to that Friday Mass – I've never missed in ten years!' Colin added, exaggerating slightly.

Jane said nothing, until Colin had enjoyed his Sunday lunch and they were relaxing together with a cup of coffee.

Then she said, 'It's only one Friday out of fifty-two, Colin. Shouldn't we be happy to welcome people from all the other traditions, and worship with them? I

know it's hard, especially for someone as faithful as
you, but they love God too, don't they? And it's certain
he loves them. Jesus prayed that we should all be one
and we know God has no favourites. So the way I see
it is that we should encourage unity all the ways we
can, even if it means a bit of sacrifice to each of us
personally.'

Colin said nothing but his face had lost its stubborn
look. When the phone rang Jane answered. 'Oh, hello,
Father', Colin heard her say. 'Oh! Well, I'm not sure.
I'll have to ask him and he'll let you know. Bye!'

'That was Father John', she said. 'He's asked if you
would read at the United Service!'

Few of us can 'go it alone' as Christians. We need one
another. Sometimes, as in the case of Colin and Jane,
married couples can help each other to see the truth.
But, married or single, we need to belong to a group,
a family, a community of some sort if we are not to
get discouraged on our journey with God.

◆━━━◆

*Next day, while they [messengers from Cornelius]
were still on their journey and had only a short dis-
tance to go before reaching Jaffa, Peter went to the
housetop at about the sixth hour to pray. He felt
hungry and was looking forward to his meal, but
before it was ready he fell into a trance and saw
heaven thrown open and something like a big sheet
being let down to earth by its four corners; it con-
tained every possible sort of animal and bird, walking,
crawling or flying ones. A voice then said to him,
'Now, Peter, kill and eat!' But Peter answered,
'Certainly not, Lord; I have never yet eaten anything
profane or unclean'. Again, a second time, the voice
spoke to him, 'What God has made clean, you have*

no right to call profane'. This was repeated three
times, and then suddenly the container was drawn up
to heaven again.

Peter was still worrying over the meaning of the
vision he had seen, when the men sent by Cornelius
arrived. They had asked where Simon's house was
and they were now standing at the door, calling out
to see if the Simon known as Peter was lodging there.
Peter's mind was still on the vision and the Spirit had
to tell him, 'Some men have come to see you. Hurry
down, and do not hesitate about going back with
them; it was I who told them to come.' Peter went
down and said to them, 'I am the man you are looking
for; why have you come?' They said, 'The centurion
Cornelius, who is an upright and God-fearing man,
highly regarded by the entire Jewish people, was
directed by a holy angel to send for you and bring you
to his house and to listen to what you have to say'.
So Peter asked them in and gave them lodging.

Next day, he was ready to go off with them,
accompanied by some of the brothers from Jaffa. They
reached Caesarea the following day, and Cornelius
was waiting for them. He had asked his relations and
close friends to be there, and as Peter reached the
house Cornelius went out to meet him, knelt at this
feet and prostrated himself. But Peter helped him up.
'Stand up,' he said, 'I am only a man after all!' Talking
together they went in to meet all the people assembled
there, and Peter said to them, 'You know it is forbid-
den for Jews to mix with people of another race and
visit them, but God has made it clear to me that I
must not call anyone profane or unclean. That is why
I made no objection to coming when I was sent for;
but I should like to know exactly why you sent for
me.' Cornelius replied, 'Three days ago I was praying
in my house at the ninth hour, when I suddenly saw

a man in front of me in shining robes. He said,
"Cornelius, your prayer has been heard and your alms
have been accepted as a sacrifice in the sight of God;
so now you must send to Jaffa and fetch Simon, known
as Peter who is lodging in the house of Simon the
tanner, by the sea". So I sent for you at once, and you
have been kind enough to come. Here we all are,
assembled in front of you, to hear what message God
has given you for us.'

Then Peter addressed them: 'The truth I have now
come to realise,' he said, 'is that God does not have
favourites, but that anybody of any nationality who
fears God and does what is right is acceptable to him.'

(Acts:9–35)

◀━▶

This is a fascinating passage, revealing the ways in
which God communicates with Peter. Through the
interpretation of a dream, Peter understands what God
wants of him. Sometimes God speaks to us in this way
and it is worth reflecting on the meaning of our
dreams. Perhaps also the attitude of Cornelius himself
is in itself a communication to Peter – here is a genuine, devout man, hungry to know more of God, and
Peter can hardly refuse to respond. So often God uses
us, weak as we are, to communicate his love to others.
And Peter's intimate 'everyday' relationship with the
Holy Spirit is something for us to wonder at. When
Peter is in a daze, the Holy Spirit tells him to hurry
downstairs and greet his visitors! So many of us are
inclined to put God in a compartment, forgetting that
he is always present with us in every situation.

There is a wonderful humility in Peter, when he is
willing to admit that God has no favourites. This was
a very difficult truth for him to swallow, brought up
as he was to think of the Jews (and therefore himself)

as God's chosen people; the elite, exclusive possessors
of the truth. There is a parallel here between the attitude of many Roman Catholics to Christians of other
traditions (and, of course, it is not only Catholics who
are guilty in this respect). We talk of non-Catholics in
a land where we are in a minority. How would we feel
if we were labelled non-Protestants?

If I don't have any close friends who are committed,
like me, to ecumenism, or justice and peace, or prayer,
I am going to be lonely and disheartened in my struggle. All of us need to belong to a group that shares our
convictions. Our world is broken and fragmented, a
place of violence, injustice and unbelief: we need to
stand together if we are to be any sort of light for this
world or leaven in its dough.

Cornelius summoned his friends and relations, and
said to Peter, 'Here we all are . . . to hear what message
God has given you for us.'

As people together we can begin to change ourselves,
and hope to change some part of our unhappy world.

FOR REFLECTION

1. Do you try to 'go it alone' as a Christian?
2. Have you sought out like-minded people in your
   parish?
3. Do you feel happy at Mass? If you do, try to discover the reasons.
4. How would you answer someone who said, 'Why
   can't we stay as we are?'

PRAYER

Lord, help me to discover where I belong, to find the
brothers and sisters who will support me and whom I
can encourage. Help me to see where change is needed

in myself, in others, and in my world, and give me the strength to work for those changes with patience, trust and love.